孔子故乡·中国山东

HOMETOWN OF CONFUCIUS, SHANDONG, CHINA

Mount Tai

刘 慧 编著 李扬眉 译

山东人民出版社
Shandong People's Publishing House

图书在版编目（CIP）数据

泰山：汉、英/刘慧编著；李扬眉译.--济南：山东人民出版社，2018.4
ISBN 978-7-209-11387-8

Ⅰ.①泰… Ⅱ.①刘… ②李… Ⅲ.①泰山-介绍-汉、英 Ⅳ.①K928.3

中国版本图书馆CIP数据核字(2018)第081843号

泰山：汉、英
刘 慧 编著 李扬眉 译

主管部门 山东出版传媒股份有限公司
出版发行 山东人民出版社
社 址 济南市英雄山路165号
邮 编 250002
电 话 总编室（0531）82098914
市场部（0531）82098027
网 址 http://www.sd-book.com.cn
印 装 北京图文天地制版印刷有限公司
经 销 新华书店

规 格 16开（170mm×240mm）
印 张 13.25
字 数 150千字
版 次 2018年4月第1版
印 次 2018年4月第1次
ISBN 978-7-209-11387-8
定 价 128.00元
如有印装质量问题，请与出版社总编室联系调换。

庄严神圣的泰山，两千年来一直是帝王朝拜的对象，其山中的人文杰作与自然景观完美和谐地融合在一起。泰山一直是中国艺术家和学者的精神源泉，是古代中国文明和信仰的象征。

——联合国教科文组织世界遗产委员会

The sacred and solemn Mount Tai had been worshipped by emperors for 2000 years, and its cultural and natural landscapes have been perfectly integrated. Since ancient times, Mount Tai has been a spiritual source for Chinese artists and scholars, as well as a symbol of ancient Chinese civilization and faith.

——The World Heritage Committee of UNESCO

Mount Tai

五嶽獨尊
昂頭天外
登峯造
萬法唯識

序言

Preface

泰山，位于中国山东省中部，巍峨壮观，神圣庄严，是中国首例世界文化与自然双遗产、世界地质公园、国家首批重点风景名胜区、AAAAA级旅游景区，享有“五岳之首”“五岳独尊”“天下第一山”等美誉。

泰山气势磅礴，以“雄”著称。主峰突兀，山势险峻，造就其拔地通天、直冲霄汉的高峻气势。周边丘陵重峦叠嶂，形成“群峰拱岱”的稳健态势。“重如泰山”“稳如泰山”“登泰山而小天下”是对泰山形态内涵的精准概括，是人们对泰山最直接的视觉感受及心理体验。

泰山风光壮丽，雄浑中兼有秀美，静穆中透着神奇。苍松巨石，云烟变幻，与巍峨山势交相辉映，使泰山风景魅力无穷。

泰山是一座人文之山。国泰民安是人们内心深处对泰山的美好寄托。历代帝王对泰山都格外尊崇，到泰山祭祀是许多帝王梦寐以求的政治夙愿。文人名士也纷至沓来，留下赞颂泰山的浩繁名篇。“泰山不让土壤”的包容性，使儒、释、道三家在这里各显千秋。泰山在赋予人们精神品格的同时，也丰厚了自身的文化意蕴。遍布山上山下的建筑、石刻，就是泰山文化史的物质载体。历史赋予了泰山特殊的文化地位，形成中华民族的认同感、归属感、向心力和凝聚力。

泰山是一座自然与文化的双重宝库，自然景观与人文杰作完美和谐交融。无论是自然的泰山，还是文化的泰山，处处散发着生命的活力，彰显出不朽的精神品格。1987年12月11日，在联合国教科文组织世界遗产委员会第11届全体会议上，泰山被正式列入世界遗产名录。

泰山是中国的，也是世界的，其文化与自然财富为人类所共享。

近年来，泰山年接待游客平均在 590 万人次左右，日均客流量 1.6 万多人。旅游高峰季节，日均客流量 4 万至 5 万人，最高时曾达到 9.2 万人。泰山国际登山节自 1987 年始，至今已成功举办 30 届；热闹的东岳庙会，年复一年地进行着；中华泰山成人礼热情迎接着不同国籍的青少年；国际历史科学大会、世界摄影大会、世界旅游发展大会等相继来到泰山；境外游客年均 30 万人次。泰山越来越被世界各国的朋友所了解，越来越显示出其独特的魅力与价值。

The grand and magnificent Mount Tai, which is located in middle Shandong Province, P.R.China, owns the titles of the first World Cultural and Natural Heritage in China, Global Geopark, the first National Key Scenic Spot, as well as AAAAA Tourist Attraction. It enjoys the reputations of "Head of the Five Sacred Mountains", the "Most Revered of the Five Sacred Mountains", and the "First Mountain under Heaven".

Geologically, Mount Tai is a tilted fault-block mountain which owns a natural momentum of rising abruptly and reaching toward the sky. It occupies a vast space with layer upon layer of hills surrounding

it, which offers a kind of imposing and steady visual perception and psychological experience described as being "heavy as Mount Tai" or "firm as Mount Tai", or "ascend the Mount Tai, all beneath the heaven appear to him small".

The beautiful landscape of Mount Tai combines grandeur with brightness, and there are miracles shining through the solemnity. With the shading of green pines and huge rocks, and changes of cloud and mist, Mount Tai presents a quite attractive scene.

As a mountain full of humanistic significance, Mount Tai bears the good wish of the country flourishing and people living in peace. Chinese emperors all showed special reverence for Mount Tai, and offering sacrifice at Mount Tai was an aspirational wish cherished by many emperors. Scholars and celebrities also visited the mountain one after another, and left a vast number of famous works that eulogize the mountain. Confucianism, Buddhism, and Taoism all have their own places due to the inclusive breadth of Mount Tai that "never refusing any minor soil". While Mount Tai enriched the spiritual characters of Chinese people, its own cultural meanings also got enriched. The architectures and steles spreading all over the mountain just embody the cultural history of Mount Tai. History endowed the mountain with special cultural position, and various wishes finally evolve into the senses of identity and belonging, as well as cohesive and centripetal force of the whole nation.

Mount Tai is a treasure perfectly integrating nature landscape and culture masterpieces. Whether the cultural Mount Tai, or the natural one, life vitality radiates from everywhere, manifesting an immortal spiritual character of the mountain. On December 11, 1987, Mount Tai was formally inscribed on the World Heritage List on the 11th Plenary Session of the UNESCO World Heritage Committee.

Mount Tai belongs not only to China, but also to the whole world, and its cultural and natural wealth is shared by all humanity. In recent years, about 5.9 million tourists visited Mount Tai every year, or over 16 thousand every day. In the peak tourist season, the daily average number is 40 to 50 thousand, and even up to 92 thousand. The International Mountaineering Festival at Mount Tai has been organized thirty sessions since 1987; the busy temple fair is held year after year; the Coming-of-age Ceremony at Mount Tai has opened to foreign countries and warmly welcomes youth from different natinalities; and the International Congress of Historical Sciences, the World Photography Conference, the World

Conference on Tourism for Development, and etc. came to Mount Tai in succession. It receives three hundred thousand tourists from abroad every year. With international recognition, the unique charm and value of Mount Tai on both culture and nature is understood and highlighted much further.

Mount Tai

目录

Contents

拔地通天

岱宗夫如何

这是一座神圣的大山。

公元前 23 至前 22 世纪，在一个春天的早上，开创中华上古文明的舜帝，登上了这座大山，手持火把点燃了堆在山巅的干柴。一股浓烟直冲云霄，随着太阳的冉冉升起，大火愈烧愈旺……

泰山之巅柴望之火
The Sacrifice Fire on the Peak of Mount Tai

舜帝画像
Portrayal of Emperor Shun

The Majestic Sight of Mount Tai

This is a sacred mountain.

One spring morning in about 23rd to 22nd century BCE, Emperor Shun who created ancient Chinese civilization, scaled the mountain and lit firewoods on the peak with his torch. A heavy smoke rose high in the sky, and the big fire burnt more and more furiously with the apperance of the sun.

虞舜泰山祭天图
Painting of Emperor Shun Offering Sacrifice to Heaven

这是文明之光，标志着中国祭天礼制的最终确立。历经几千年薪传，圣火在中国人的心中从来不曾熄灭过。

这座大山就是泰山。

这一历史片段，被详细地记录在中国最早的一部历史文献《尚书》中。

That was the glory of civilization, which marked the final establishment of the ritual system of sacrifice to Heaven in China. The sacred fire had been passed on for thousand of years, and never quenches in the hearts of Chinese people.

The mountain is Mount Tai.

And the historical episode was detailed in the *Book of Documents*, the earliest Chinese historical documents.

桓圭。侯執信圭。伯執躬圭。子執穀璧。男執蒲璧。是圭璧爲五等之瑞。諸侯執之以爲王者瑞信。故稱瑞也。舜以朔日受終於文祖。又徧祭羣神。及斂五瑞。則入月以多日矣。盡以正月中。謂從斂瑞以後至月末也。乃日日見四岳及九州牧監。舜初攝位。當發號出令。日日見之。與之言也。州牧各監一州諸侯。故言監也。更復還五瑞於諸侯者。此瑞本受於堯。斂而又還之。若言舜新付之。改爲舜臣。與之正新君之始也。

歲二月。東巡守。至于岱宗。柴。傳 諸侯爲天子守土。故稱守巡行之。既班瑞之明月。乃順春東巡。岱宗泰山。爲四岳所宗。燔柴祭天告至。望秩于山川。傳 東岳諸侯境內名山大川。如其秩次望祭之。謂五岳牲禮視三公。四瀆視諸侯。其餘視伯子男。肆覲東后。傳 遂見東方之國君。協時月。正日。同律度量衡。傳 合四時之氣節。月之大小。日之甲乙。使齊一也。律法制。及尺丈斛斗斤兩皆均同。

乾隆四年校刊　尚書注疏卷二　舜典　十一

《尚书·舜典》
The Cannon of Shun in the *Book of Documents*

雄伟的泰山
The Magnificent Mount Tai

中国首例世界双遗产

The First World Cultural and Natural Heritage in China

泰山，由于特殊的地学构造，其主峰——玉皇顶高耸突起，海拔 1545 米，与山下平原有着 1300 多米的相对高差，在方圆数百公里的范围内“一山独尊”，给人以“拔地通天”的直观感受。

Mount Tai, due to special geological structure, the Jade Emperor Peak rises abruptly to 1,545 metres (5,068 ft) above sea level, and a relative height difference of more than 1,300 metres with the submontane plain. As the only peak within hundreds of kilometers around, the mountain makes a strong impression of "rising straight and reaching toward the sky".

19 世纪"拔地通天"刻石
The Stele "Rising Straight and Heaven-Reaching" in the 19th Century

山高云海静
High Mountain and Tranquil Sea of Clouds

泰山
Mount Tai

瞻鲁台　The Lu-viewing Platform

在中国第一部诗歌总集——《诗经》中，就说“泰山岩岩，鲁邦所詹”。“岩岩”，是对泰山体躯雄浑的感受。“鲁邦所詹”，是对泰山之尊的认知。

In the *Book of Poetry,* the oldest existing collection of Chinese poetry, it says: “Lofty is Mount Tai, Looked up from Lu State.” The former part of the sentence describes the marvel of the mountain, while the latter part states the cognition of its honor.

“泰山岩岩，鲁邦所詹”
“Lofty is Mount Tai, Looked up from Lu State”

20 世纪“中华泰山”刻石
The Stele “Mount Tai of China” in the 20th Century

16 世纪 “五岳独宗”碑刻
The Stele “Most Revered of the Five Sacred Mountains” in the 16th Century

泰山，在中国人的心目中有着至高无上的地位。它是中华民族的精神之山，是中国礼制与尊严的象征，承载了一个民族对和平和谐、国泰民安的希冀。“泰山安则四海皆安”，泰山所坐落的城市——泰安，便是因此而得名并沿用至今。

Mount Tai enjoys a supreme status in the minds of Chinese people. As the peak representing the spirit of Chinese nation, it not only symbolizes the Chinese rites, but also bears the nation's hope for peace, harmony, and prosperity. “If Mount Tai is stable, so is the entire country.”Tai'an, the city where Mount Tai is located, was thus named (both characters “*tai*” and “*an*”have the independent meaning of “peace”) and remains ever since.

世界遗产委员会专家卢卡斯先生考察泰山
Mr. Lucas, Expert of the World Heritage Committee Visiting Mount Tai

泰山是中华民族的骄傲，也是全人类的共同财富。

1987 年 12 月 11 日，泰山被正式批准列入世界遗产名录单。时任联合国教科文组织总干事的费德里科·马约尔，签署了世界遗产证书：

世界遗产委员会将泰山列入世界遗产名录。

泰山是全人类共同保护的具有突出和普遍价值的文化和自然遗产。

Mount Tai is not only the pride of China, but also the common wealth shared by the whole world.

On December 11, 1987, Mount Tai was formally inscribed on the World Heritage List. Then Director-General of UNESCO Federico Mayor signed the certificate:

The World Heritage Committeeh as inscribed Mount Taishan on the World Heritage List.

Inscription on this List confirms the exceptional and universal value of a cultural or natural site which requires protection for the benefit of all humanity.

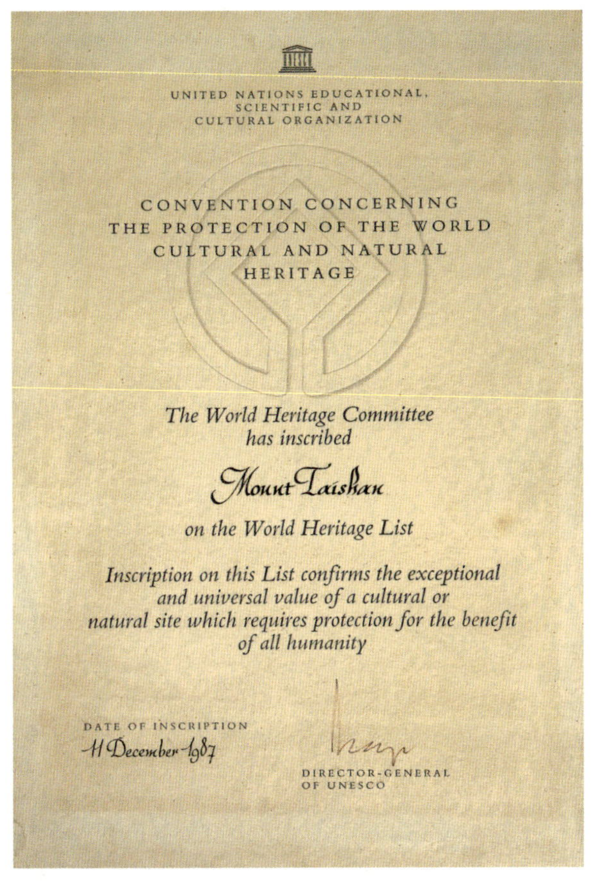

UNITED NATIONS EDUCATIONAL,
SCIENTIFIC AND
CULTURAL ORGANIZATION

CONVENTION CONCERNING
THE PROTECTION OF THE WORLD
CULTURAL AND NATURAL
HERITAGE

The World Heritage Committee
has inscribed

Mount Taishan

on the World Heritage List

Inscription on this List confirms the exceptional
and universal value of a cultural or
natural site which requires protection for the benefit
of all humanity

DATE OF INSCRIPTION
11 December 1987

DIRECTOR-GENERAL
OF UNESCO

泰山世界遗产证书
The “World Heritage Certificate” for Mount Tai

中国成为《保护世界文化和自然遗产公约》缔约国之后，泰山成为中国首例世界文化和自然双遗产。

After China became one party of *Convention concerning the Protection of the World Cultural and Natural Heritage*, Mount Tai becomes the first wold cultural natural heritage in China.

泰山是一座“大山”

Mount Tai, a Great Mountain

泰山，也称“太山”。大山、太山、泰山，都是对这座山的称谓。泰山或曰“岱宗”“岱岳”，也均来自于大山之“大”。

Mount Tai is also known as Daizong or Daishan, and all the names refer to the “grandness” of Mount Tai.

16 世纪“首出万山”刻石
The Stele “Head of Mountains” in the 16th Century

18 世纪初“惟天为大”刻石
The Stele “Only the Heaven, Only the Grandness” in the Early 18th Century

16 世纪 “万代瞻仰”碑刻
The Stone Inscription “Worshipped by All the Ages” in the 16th Century

泰山“以大为尊”，主要还在于它的文化之“大”。春秋战国时期，诸子蜂起，百家争鸣，但泰山始终是崇高、大美的象征。

Mount Tai is respected for its grandness, and principally for its grandness on culture. Throughout the times from the Spring and Autumn period to the Warring States period when philosophers and various schools arose, Mount Tai remained to be a symbol of sublimity and great beauty.

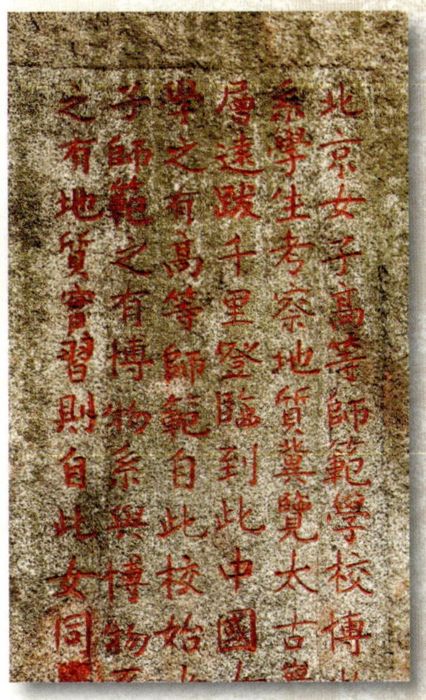

泰山地质刻石
The Geological Rock Inscription of Mount Tai

章鸿钊先生
Mr. Zhang Hongzhao

地球档案

Archives of the Earth

1922 年，一位地质学家在泰山朝阳洞山谷的一处摩崖刻石竣工。泰山刻石数以千计，但作为地质刻石，前无古人。

In the year of 1922, a geologist completed one rock inscription in the valley of Chaoyang Cave. There are thousands of inscribed rocks on Mount Tai, yet it is an unprecedented one as a geological rock inscription.

这位地质学家，便是中国近代地质学奠基人之一的章鸿钊先生（1877—1951）。他在泰山考察期间，留下了这具有里程碑意义的地质石刻。

自 20 世纪初，中国地质学家陆续来泰山考察。而在此之前，俄国、德国、美国、法国等地质学家，都曾来过泰山“寻宝”。

……

This geologist is one of the founders of modern geology in China, Mr. Zhang Hongzhao(1877-1951CE). He left the geological stele as a milestone during his investigation of Mount Tai.

Since the early 20th century, Chinese geologists had successively come to Mount Tai for investigation. And before then, geologists from Russia, Germany, America, and France had ever visited the mountain for treasure hunts.

最早来泰山做地质考察的德国地理、地质学家李希霍芬先生
The German Geographer and Geologist Richthofen Who Came to Mount Tai for Geological Surveying

泰山世界地质公园标志碑
The “Global Geopark” Monument on Mount Tai

重力崩塌——“烟横云倚”　Gravity Collapse: Collapsed Site in Swinging and Varied Cloud

构造断层——云步桥断崖　Structural Fault: the Bluff on the Cloud Step Bridge

奇觀

流水侵蚀——天井湾崖层
Flowing Water Erosion: Cliff Stratums in the Heavenly Well Bay

岩体侵入——彩石溪岩体
Rock Intrusion: Rocks in the Colorful Rock Stream

泰山地质，是地球不可或缺的一份履历。

2007 年，泰山入选世界地质公园。

The geology of Mount Tai is an indispensable record of the earth.

Mount Tai was honored "Global Geopark" in 2007.

重力崩塌——"奇观"刻石
Gravity Collapse: the "Spectacle" Stele

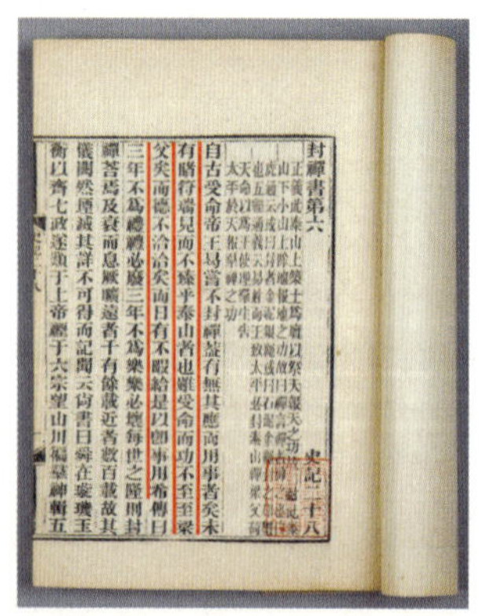

《史记·封禅书》书影
"Treatise on the Sacrifice to Heaven and Earth" in *Records of the Grand Historian*

帝王的封禅祭祀
Sacrifices to Heaven and Earth by Emperors

在中国历史上，最神圣、最隆重的祭祀仪式是泰山封禅大典。所谓封禅，就是在泰山祭天祭地。与一般祭祀天地的仪式不同，它是国家统一、众生安泰的标志。

In Chinese history, the ceremony of sacrifices to Heaven and Earth at Mount Tai had always been the most sacred and solemn one. Different from general rites of offering sacrifices to Heaven and Earth, it is a symbol of national unity and peaceful lives.

秦始皇画像
Portrayal of Qin Shi Huang

泰山封禅第一人——秦始皇

Qin Shi Huang: the First Person Offering Sacrifices to Heaven and Earth at Mount Tai

封禅，是战国末年人们希望有一位君主能统一天下，结束长期战乱而形成的一种政治愿望。秦始皇嬴政（前259—前210），建立了中国历史上第一个统一的多民族的中央集权国家，始称"皇帝"。"书同文，车同轨"，统一度量衡，奠定了封建社会的基础。

公元前219年，秦始皇不远千里，从西安咸阳向着泰山跋涉而来。在泰山之巅，他用旧时秦国祭祀上帝的礼仪祭天，在山下的小山梁父山祭地，完成了历史上的第一次封禅大典。

The sacrifices to Heaven and Earth is a kind of political desire formed in the late Warring States period that people expected for a sovereign ending the long-term chaos. Qin Shi Huang (i.e. the First Emperor of Qin Dynasty) named Ying Zheng (259-210 BCE) established the first unified, multi-national, and centralized country in Chinese history. Unification of the Chinese characters as well as standardization of the Chinese units of measurements such as weights, measures, and the length of the axles of carts (so every cart could run smoothly in the ruts of the new roads) laid the foundation of imperial China.

In 219 BCE, Qin Shi Huang travelled a long distance from Xianyang City, Shaanxi to Mount Tai. He offered sacrifice to Heaven following former rites of the State of Qin on the mountain peak, and the one to Earth on a lower hill named Liangfu, thus completed the first ceremony of sacrifices to Heaven and Earth in Chinese history.

秦始皇数次出巡，多次刻石以铭功颂德。其中最有名的是秦泰山刻石。后又由秦二世再刻，计222字，到清代时只剩下10个残字。字体为小篆，由丞相李斯所书，用笔劲秀圆健，结构严谨，堪称秦篆的代表作，是秦王朝统一文字的见证。此刻石可谓泰山刻石的滥觞，现收藏于山下的岱庙。

秦泰山刻石残存十字本拓片
The Ten-character Stele Rubbing of Qin on Mount Tai

In his visits outside, Qin Shi Huang made lots of stone inscriptions to sing the praise of himself, among which the stele on Mount Tai is the most famous one. The stele was inscribed again under the command of the Second Emperor of Qin afterwards, totaling 222 characters, yet only 10 fragmentary characters were left till the Qing Dynasty. The epigraph was written in Xiaozhuan style (Small Seal Script) by the Prime Minister Li Si with firm strokes and rigorous structure, which could be regarded as master work of Small Seal Script as well as a witness of character unification by the Qin Dynasty. As the origin of steles on Mount Tai, it is now preserved in the Dai Temple.

现存岱庙的秦泰山刻石
The Qin Stele on Mount Tai in the Dai Temple

"五大夫"松
Fifth Rank Pine

秦始皇在封禅结束后下山时，遇到暴风雨，躲避于一棵松树下。此树因护驾有功，被封为"五大夫"。如今的"五大夫松"，仍在荫庇着来来往往的过客。

Qin Shi Huang met stormy weather when going downhill after the sacrifice ceremony, and took shelter under a pine. This pine was granted the title "Fifth Rank Pine" for successfully escorting the emperor. Today, it still shades the passing travelers.

秦始皇避雨图
Painting of Qin Shi Huang Taking Shelter from the Storm

唐高宗皇帝画像
Portrayal of Emperor Gaozong of Tang

武则天皇帝画像
Portrayal of Empress Wu Zetian

标新立异的“二圣”
——唐高宗与武则天

Two Unconventional Sages: Emperor Gaozong of Tang and Wu Zetian

“二圣”是唐高宗与武则天的并称。唐高宗（628—683）于公元649年即位。武则天（624—705）于公元690年登上王位，是中国历史上唯一的女皇帝。

The “two sages” are the combined name of Emperor Gaozong of the Tang Dynasty and Wu Zetian. Emperor Gaozong (628-683 CE) ascended the throne in 649 CE, and Wu Zetian(624-705 CE), the only empress in Chinese history, ascended the throne in 690 CE.

公元665年12月，唐高宗的封禅大军到达泰山，封禅仪式在有条不紊中进行。与历史上秦始皇、汉武帝、汉光武帝封禅最大的不同是，武则天参与了祭祀典礼。女性跻身泰山封禅大典，这在中国历史上是唯一的一次。

In December 665 CE, the retinue of Emperor Gaozong of Tang arrived Mount Tai for sacrifices to Heaven and Earth, and the ceremony proceeded in an orderly way. A major difference of this ceremony with the ones offered by Qin Shi Huang, Emperor Wu of Han, and Emperor Guangwu of Han is that Wu Zetian attended the ceremony. It is the only time in Chinese history that a woman was among the sacrifices to Heaven and Earth.

“二圣”双尊图
Painting of the “Two Sages”

记载武则天遣员来泰山祭祀的“双束碑”
The Parallel Steles Recording Wu Zetian Dispatching Officials to Mount Tai for Sacrifice

武则天对封禅的“立异”，引来唐玄宗为大唐进行拨乱反正之举。公元 725 年，唐玄宗“受命中兴”，封禅泰山。

Wu Zetian's unconventional act made Emperor Xuanzong of Tang decided to "bring things back to order" for the dynasty. In 725 CE, Emperor Xuanzong was committed to undertake the reviving of the Tang Dynasty, and he also offered sacrifices to Heaven and Earth at Mount Tai.

唐玄宗泰山封禅图
Painting of Emperor Xuanzong of Tang Offering Sacrifices to Heaven and Earth

来泰山最多的皇帝——乾隆

Emperor Qianlong of Qing: the Emperor Visiting Mount Tai the Most Times

在历代帝王的亲临祭祀中，来泰山次数最多、所留遗迹最丰的，要属清代的乾隆皇帝（1711—1799）。

从 1736 年即位，到 1796 年退位的 60 年间，乾隆皇帝先后到泰山 10 次，列皇帝到泰山次数的历史之最。

Among the emperors who came to Mount Tai for sacrifices in person, Emperor Qianlong (1711-1799 CE) of the Qing Dynasty visited the most times and left richest relics.

During sixty years from ascending the throne in 1736 CE to abdicating in 1796 CE, Emperor Qianlong visited Mount Tai ten times, the highest in history.

乾隆皇帝画像
Portrayal of Emperor Qianlong of Qing

1748 年，乾隆皇帝祭祀泰山神的盛典在岱庙隆重举行。躬祀泰山神的仪式中，乾隆皇帝行“两跪六叩之礼”。仪程严谨，气氛庄重。

In 1748 CE, the grand ceremony of Emperor Qianlong offering sacrifice to the God of Mount Tai was held at the Dai Temple in rigorous procedure and solemn atmosphere. The emperor performed thrice kowtow and nine times prostration in the ceremony.

岱庙配天门——乾隆皇帝曾于此处盥洗
The Peitian Gate in the Dai Temple, Where Emperor Qianlong Washed Face and Hands

乾隆所留《朝阳洞诗》摩崖刻石，有“万丈碑”之称。山下的岱庙、山上的碧霞祠等，都因在乾隆时期重修，得以保存完整。

The stele engraved “Poem on the Chaoyang Cave” written by Emperor Qianlong is also known as the “lofty stele”. The relics such as the Palace of Heavenly Blessings and the Shrine of the Blue Dawn are all well preserved due to the renovation in the reign of Emperor Qianlong.

乾隆皇帝《朝阳洞诗》刻石如钤印在泰山上的一枚图章
The Stele Engraved "Poem on the Chaoyang Cave" by Emperor Qianlong Seems Like a Seal Stamped on Mount Tai

文人名士的泰山情结

The "Mount Tai Complex" among Literati and Celebrities

“高山仰止，景行行止。” 无数的文人士大夫，竞相登览这座充满人文情怀的大山。

"The mountain towers into the sky, the roads in front of us lie." Numerous scholars, literati, and bureaucrats came to visit the mountain full of humanistic feelings.

孔子登泰山而小天下

“Confucius Ascended the Mount Tai, and All beneath the Heaven Appeared to Him Small”

孔子（前 551—前 479），是中国的圣人。孟子曰：“孔子登东山而小鲁，登泰山而小天下。”这是一种文化巡礼。

Confucius (551-479 BCE) is the sage of China. Mencius said that “Confucius ascended the Eastern Hill, and the State of Lu appeared to him small; while he ascended the Mount Tai, and all beneath the Heaven appeared to him small.” That is a kind of cultural pilgrimage.

孔子像
Portrayal of Confucius

在世人的眼里，孔子可以与泰山类比。而在孔子的眼里，泰山则是礼制的象征，是神圣而不可冒犯的。

To the Chinese people, Confucius can equal to Mount Tai; while in Confucius' eyes, Mount Tai is the symbol of sacred rites.

中外青少年在“孔子小天下处”碑前留影
Chinese and foreign teenagers Took Group Photo before the Stele

“登高必自”碑
The Inscription “DengGaoBiZi” (literally “In ascending a height, we must start from a lower place”)

“孔登岩”刻石
The Stele “Rock of Confucius’Accession”

从山下拾级而上，“孔子登临处”“孔子崖”“望吴胜迹”“孔子庙”“孔登岩”等景观，寄托着人们对孔子的敬仰之心。

On the ascent from the foot of the mountain, the landscapes such as “Point of Confucius’ Accession”, “Confucius Cliff”, “Site for Overlooking Wu State”, “Temple of Confucius”, and the stele “Rock of Confucius’ Accession”, all express admiration for Confucius.

"望吴胜迹""孔子庙"石坊
Stone Archways of "Temple of Confucius" and "Site for Overlooking Wu State"

孔子庙门联——"仰之弥高，钻之弥坚，可以语上也；出乎其类，拔乎其萃，宜若登天然"
Couplets on the Temple of Confucius, literally means: "The more you have looked up to it the higher it appears, the more you have tried to penetrate into it the more impenetrable it seems to be; those people may be spoken of high things. The sages stand out of their fellows, and rise above the level; to learn them may well be likened to ascending the Heaven."

孔子庙东配殿楹联——“泰山岳中之孔子，孔子人中之泰山”
Couplets on the East Side Hall of the Temple of Confucius: “Mount Tai, Confucius in mountains; Confucius, Mount Tai among people.”

杜甫《望岳》

岱宗夫如何？齐鲁青未了。
造化钟神秀，阴阳割昏晓。
荡胸生层云，决眦入归鸟。
会当凌绝顶，一览众山小。

杜甫望岳图
Painting of Du Fu Gazing on Mount Tai

杜甫（712—770），是中国唐代伟大的现实主义诗人，被尊称为“诗圣”。他的诗歌《望岳》，已成千古绝唱。

Du Fu (712-770 CE), the great realistic poet of the Tang Dynasty, is honored the “Saint of Poem”. His “Gazing on Mount Tai” has been a masterpiece through the ages.

Du Fu's Poem "Gazing on Mount Tai"

And what then is Daizong like? –
over Qi and Lu, green unending.
Creation compacted spirit splendors here,
Dark and light, riving dusk and dawn.
Exhilarating the breast, it produces layers of cloud;
splitting eye-pupils, it has homing birds entering.
Someday may I climb up to its highest summit,
with one sweeping view see how small all other mountains are.

"阴阳割昏晓"
"Dark and Light, Riving Dusk and Dawn"

"青未了""割昏晓""入归鸟""众山小"，诗人对泰山的感受，完全融入可视的形象之中。

"Green unending", "riving dusk and dawn", "homing birds entering", "how small all other mountains are", the poet's feelings of Mount Tai are fully integrated into visual images.

“一览众山小”
“One Sweeping View See How Small All Other Mountains Are”

山上山下，有杜甫的《望岳》诗石刻多处，真、草、隶、篆，皆具意韵。让游人在领略诗人心境的同时，也感受到在千年之间文人往来的持续用心。

From the foot to the top, there are many steles engraved Du Fu’s “Gazing on Mount Tai” written in various calligraphy styles of regular script, cursive script, clerical script, seal script, and etc. with various artistic charms. While appreciating the poet’s mood, tourists can also feel the unremitting and sincere echoes among literati over thousand years.

1983 年岱顶《望岳》刻石
The Stele "Gazing on Mount Tai" on the Summit (1983)

李白"朝饮"的王母池
The Mother Queen Pool Where Li Bai Drank in the Morning

"天关"——南天门
The "Gate to Heaven": the South Gate to Heaven

李白寻仙

Li Bai "Seeking Immortals"

朝饮王母池，暝投天门关。

独抱绿绮琴，夜行青山间。

Drinking by the Mother Queen Pool at dawn,
Till the dusk I arrived the Gate to Heaven.
Alone holding my gorgeous zither,
I went night walk in the green mountain.

公元 742 年 4 月的某一天，42 岁的诗人李白登临泰山。从山下的王母池启程，沿着唐高宗、唐玄宗登封泰山的御道攀缘而上，黄昏时分抵达南天门，仙游便由此开始……

One day in April 742 CE, the 42-year-old poet Li Bai climbed Mount Tai. He started his fairy tour from the Mother Queen Pool at the foot of the mountain, went up along the pass used by Emperor Gaozong and Emperor Xuanzong, and arrived at the South Gate to Heaven at dusk.

Mount Tai

“攀崖上日观，伏槛窥东暝”
“Climbing Cliffs to the Sun Viewing Peak, Bending over the Sill to Watch Evening Twilight in the East”

“长松入云汉，远望不盈尺”
“The Tall Pine Reaching the Sky, Less Than One Chi Looking from Afar”

“精神四飞扬，如出天地间”
“The Spirit Soaring All around, Like Galloping between the Heaven and Earth”

李白（701—762），是中国唐代伟大的浪漫主义诗人，被尊称为“诗仙”。

此次仙游，李白写了《游泰山诗》六首。诗人用他豪放的风格、瑰玮的意象，给泰山带来了灵动与飘逸。

Li Bai (701-762 CE), known as the “Immortal Poet”, is a great romantic poet of the Tang Dynasty.

In this tour, Li Bai wrote “Poems on the Visit to Mount Tai” composed of six pieces. The poet brought Mount Tai ethereality and elegance with his generous style and magnificent fantasy.

“天门一长啸，万里清风来。”李白豪气的流动，永恒不息。

“A long, long whistle at the Gate to Heaven, Summons refreshing breeze from far, far away.” Li Bai’s heroic spirit flows eternally.

国之瑰宝——泰山祭器

Treasures of the Country: Sacrificial Utensils of Mount Tai

泰山祭器，主要来自于中国古代的皇宫，代表了当时最先进的生产、工艺水平。

The sacrificial utensils of Mount Tai mainly come from the palace in imperial China, which represent the highest level of craftsmanship at that time.

黄釉青花葫芦瓶

The Yellow-Glazed Gourd-shaped Bottle

泰山镇山三宝之一。乾隆皇帝于 1787 年御赐岱庙。通体以黄釉为底色，饰青花缠枝莲纹，瓶底有“大明嘉靖年制”楷书青花款。

As one of the three treasures guarding Mount Tai, this article was bestowed to the Dai Temple by Emperor Qianlong in 1787 CE. The entire body of the bottle is covered by yellow glaze, decorated with blue-and-white interlaced lotus design, and marked the blue-and-white inscription “Made in the Reign of Jiajing of Ming” in regular script at the bottom.

黄釉青花葫芦瓶
The Yellow-Glazed Gourd-shaped Bottle

温凉玉圭

The Warm and Cool Jade

泰山镇山三宝之一。乾隆皇帝于1771年以为母亲贺寿的名义颁赐岱庙。玉圭在中国礼制中，是权力的象征。圭为玉质，故称“玉圭”。用手触摸，上下温度感略异，俗称“温凉玉”。

As one of the three treasures guarding Mount Tai, this jade was bestowed to the Dai Temple by Emperor Qianlong in the name of congratulating his mother's birthday in 1771 CE. The kind of tablet made out of jade is a symbol of power. It is nicknamed "warm and cool jade", because its upper part and lower part vary slightly in temperature.

沉香狮子

Eaglewood Lions

泰山镇山三宝之一。乾隆皇帝于 1762 年御赐岱庙。系用沉香木的天然形态雕刻粘合而成。

As one of the three treasures guarding Mount Tai, this sculpture was bestowed to the Dai Temple by Emperor Qianlong in 1762 CE, which was engraved and conglutinated conforming to the natural form of the eaglewood piece.

庙会启动仪式
Opening Ceremony of the Temple Fair

多彩民俗
Colorful Folk Customs

泰山，有皇帝的作为，有文人的灵光，也有平民百姓自由想象的张扬。

There are emperor's actions, literati's brightness, and free imaginations of common people coexisting on Mount Tai.

开城门仪式
The Gate Opening Ceremony

岱庙壁画中帝王之仪的泰山神
The God of Mount Tai in an Emperor's Appearance on the Dai Temple Frescoes

大山之神——东岳大帝

Great Deity of Mount Tai: God of the Grand Mountain

东岳大帝，被尊为泰山神，是生命之神。这生的大幸与不幸，不仅限于人的个体，也包括一个国家的存亡。

尊重生命，生生不息，正是泰山信仰的本质所在。

The Great Deity of Mount Tai is honored the God of Mount Tai and the God of Life. The fortune and misfortune of life is not limited to individuals, but also includes the preservation or destruction of a country.

Respecting life in an endless succession is just the essence of belief on Mount Tai.

乾隆皇帝所题“大德曰生”匾额
The Board "Great Virtue Calls Life" inscribed by Emperor Qianlong of Qing

康熙皇帝所题“配天作镇”匾额
The Board "Matching the Heaven and Guarding the Place" inscribed by Emperor Kangxi of Qing

泰山神曾受到历代皇帝的加封，唐代封为“天齐王”，宋代晋封为“天齐仁圣帝”。在岱庙天贶殿的壁画上，可一睹这位“圣帝”的风采。

The God of Mount Tai had been granted many titles by emperors in successive dynasties, such as the “King Equaling Heaven” in the Tang Dynasty, and the “Benevolent Sage King Equaling Heaven” in the Song Dynasty. The elegant demeanor of the “sage emperor” can be seen on the frescoes in the Palace of Heavenly Blessings of the Dai Temple.

清光绪（1871—1908）东岳大帝画像
Portrayal of the Great Deity of Mount Tai in the Reign of Emperor Guangxu of Qing (1871–1908 CE)

清光绪（1871—1908）东岳大帝正宫——淑明后画像
Portrayal of Empress Shuming, Wife of the Great Deity of Mount Tai in the Reign of Emperor Guangxu of Qing(1871–1908CE)

神界女皇——碧霞元君

Goddess of the Blue Dawn: Empress of Divinity

碧霞元君，是道教给予泰山女神的道号。在民间，人们称这位女神：泰山娘娘、泰山奶奶、泰山老母。

The Goddess of the Blue Dawn is the Taoist name of the Goddess of Mount Tai. She also has the folk names of "Lady of Mount Tai", "Grandma of Mount Tai", and "Mother of Mount Tai".

明万历（1573—1620）御制碧霞元君、眼光娘娘、送子娘娘画像
Portrayals of the Goddess of the Blue Dawn, Goddess of Eyesight, and Goddess of Fertility in the Reigh of Emperor Wanli of Ming (1573–1620 CE)

清代（1644—1912）民间碧霞元君——泰山圣母画像

Folk Portrayal of the Goddess of the Blue Dawn, i.e. the Goddess of Mount Tai in the Qing Dynasty (1644-1912 CE)

碧霞元君信仰的兴盛，大致经历了从民间到宫廷、从宫廷再到民间这样一个过程。碧霞元君信仰的最初形成，则来源于人们对生育需求的愿望。

The rise of the Goddess of the Blue Dawn belief experienced the course of developing from folk society to the court, and then returning to folk society from the court. And the initial formation of the belief was derived from the desire for fertility.

清代（1644—1912）民间送子娘娘画像
Folk Portrayal of the Goddess of Fertility in the Qing Dynasty

清代（1644—1912）
民间眼光奶奶画像
Folk Portrayal of the Goddess of Eyesight in the Qing Dynasty

平安使者——泰山石敢当

Shi Gandang of Mount Tai: Messenger of Safeness

泰山脚下的村落，在房舍或街巷要冲常能看到“泰山石敢当”刻石，人们用之以镇宅辟邪。

The kind of “Shi Gandang of Mount Tai” stele can often be seen in rural houses, streets, lanes, and gateways at the foot of Mount Tai, used for guarding the house and exorcising evil spirit.

以石为镇，以石为安。对石头的崇拜，是山岳崇拜的延伸和发展。泰山是镇国之山，可“配天作镇”，威力最大，所以泰山石敢当成为镇邪祟、保平安的最佳选择。

The worship of stone is the continuation and development of the worship of mountain. As the peak guarding the whole country, Mount Tai owns the greatest power which can “match the Heaven and guard the place”, so Shi Gandang of Mount Tai becomes the best choice in expelling the evil thing and protecting the safeness.

在北京的天坛公园，于祈年殿东南向放置有“七星石”，它是京都的泰山石敢当。

In the Temple of Heaven in Beijing, the Seven-star stone group lies in southeast of the Hall of Prayer for Good Harvests. Those stones are Shi Gandang in the capital.

北京天坛公园内的“七星石”
The Seven-star Stone Group in the Temple of Heaven in Beijing

四川桃坪羌寨泰山石敢当
Shi Gandang in a Qiang Stockade Village, Taoping, Sichuan Province

安徽徽州泰山石敢当
Shi Gandang in Huizhou, Anhui Province

山东济南泰山石敢当
Shi Gandang of Mount Tai in Jinan, Shandong Province

石敢当纯朴的平安观念，得到了不同区域、不同民族广泛的文化认同，使之成为泰山平安的使者，足迹遍布海内外。

The simple idea to ensure safeness contained in Shi Gandang gains wide acceptance of different areas and nationalities. Bearing the role of messenger of safeness, Shi Gandang has spread its footprints home and abroad.

泰山石敢当信仰习俗，2006 年经国务院批准列入第一批国家级非物质文化遗产名录。

The belief of Shi Gandang was included in the first batch of national intangible cultural heritage by the State Council of the People's Republic of China in 2006.

日本冲绳石敢当
Shi Gandang in Okinawa, Japan

越南泰山石敢当
Shi Gandang in Vietnam

民间的狂欢节——东岳庙会

Temple Fair of the Eastern Peak: the Folk Carnival

人们在创造出让自己百般信赖的神祇的同时，也为自己心灵的自由洞开了一扇窗户。

庙会是民间信仰的舞台，平民百姓是这场生活大戏的主角。

新春伊始，人们从四面八方涌入庙中，兑现往年的期许，带回新一年的愿望。

While people create god to be sincerely trusted, they also open a window for the freedom of their soul.

Temple Fair is the stage of folk belief, and common people are the leading roles of this living opera.

At the beginning of the Spring Festival, people surge into the temple from all sides for fulfilling expectations of the past year, and making wishes for a new year.

挤满了盘道的进香队伍
Pilgrims Crowding on the Stairs

心灵圣殿
Temple for the Soul

进香许愿之一
Offering Incense and Making Wishes Ⅰ

进香许愿之二
Offering Incense and Making Wishes Ⅱ

进香许愿之三
Offering Incense and Making Wishes Ⅲ

听山东快书
Enjoying the Shandong Clapper Ballad

品小调
Appreciating the Ditties

庙会，同样也是一次文化的盛会。

The temple fair is also a cultural pageant.

庙市场景之一
One Corner of the Temple Fair I

庙市场景之二
One Corner of the Temple Fair II

看大戏
Watching the Opera

不懈的登攀者——挑山工

1981 年，中国作家冯骥才先生创作泰山《挑山工》一文。该文先后选入全国高中、小学语文课本，让数以亿计的人们知道了泰山挑山工。

坚韧——攀登——目标，激励着人们的毅力和勇气，为达到目标而不懈努力。

在泰山脚下的大津口乡，一位姓孙的挑山工，靠着一双坚实的臂膀，将儿子“挑”成了这个乡唯一的博士。

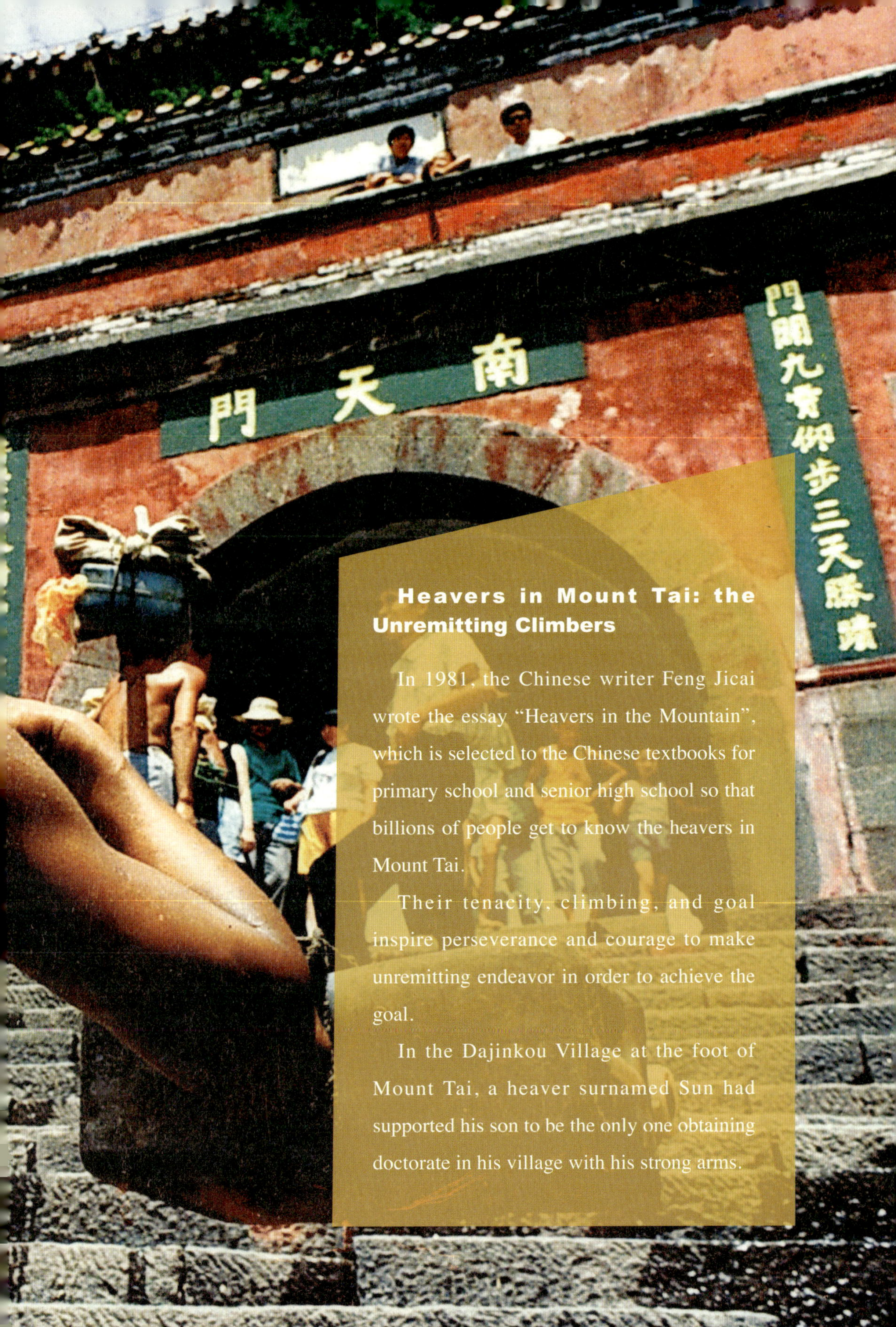

Heavers in Mount Tai: the Unremitting Climbers

In 1981, the Chinese writer Feng Jicai wrote the essay "Heavers in the Mountain", which is selected to the Chinese textbooks for primary school and senior high school so that billions of people get to know the heavers in Mount Tai.

Their tenacity, climbing, and goal inspire perseverance and courage to make unremitting endeavor in order to achieve the goal.

In the Dajinkou Village at the foot of Mount Tai, a heaver surnamed Sun had supported his son to be the only one obtaining doctorate in his village with his strong arms.

杨辛、钱绍武先生与挑山工亲切交谈
Mr. Yang Xin and Qian Shaowu Talked with the Heavers

挑山，是值得尊敬的一个行当。中国当代美学家杨辛先生、雕塑家钱绍武先生义卖作品成立泰山“三工”（挑山工、护林工、环卫工）基金，以表达崇敬与感激之情。

Carrying goods in mountain is a respectable profession. To express their reverence and gratitude, contemporary Chinese esthetician Yang Xin and sculpturer Qian Shaowu saled part of their works for establishing a fund for three kinds of workers in Mount Tai, i.e. the heavers, forest rangers, and sanitation workers.

冯骥才先生的国画《挑山工》
Traditional Chinese Painting “Heaver in Mount Tai” by Mr.Feng Jicai

脊梁
Backbones

造化钟神秀

Natural Miracle and Beauty of Mount Tai

自然的泰山，自有自然的神奇。基于它的纬度、它的地质，顶天立地，气贯长虹。

The natural Mount Tai owns natural miracles. Its geographic position and characteristics had made a grand and sublime momentum of the mountain.

光色的交响
Symphony of Light and Color

旭日东升
The Rising Sun

视觉盛宴——旭日东升

Visual Feast: the Rising Sun from the East

清代散文家姚鼐所撰《登泰山记》，生动地描绘出泰山极顶日出之时的雄浑景象。1924 年，印度大文豪泰戈尔访华前夕，《小说月报》要出“泰戈尔专号”，中国诗人徐志摩应主编郑振铎之邀撰写了《泰山日出》一文。

The marvelous scene of sunrise at the summit of Mount Tai is vividly described in the prose “A Travel to Mount Tai” written by essayist Yao Nai of the Qing Dynasty. On the eve of Tagore’s visit to China in 1924, the journal Novelty Monthly schemed a “Special Issue of Tagore”, and Chinese poet Xu Zhimo wrote the article “Sunrise at Mount Tai” at the invitation of the editor-in-chief Zheng Zhenduo.

春之云海日出
The Sea of Clouds and the Sunrise in Spring

Mount Tai

登泰山看日出，自古就是游人理想的选择。不同的季节，不同的气象，异彩纷呈。

“东方红，太阳升。”泰山日出是视觉的盛宴，更是一种文化上的心理共鸣。

Climbing Mount Tai and watching the sunrise has always been an ideal choice for tourists since ancient times. Different seasons and climates bring Mount Tai varied colourful splendour.

“Red Sun rises in the East.” Sunrise at Mount Tai is not only a kind of visual feast, but also a psychological resonance on culture.

秋之云海日出
The Sea of Clouds and the Sunrise in Autumn

夏之云海日出
The Sea of Clouds and the Sunrise in Summer

冬之云海日出
The Sea of Clouds and the Sunrise in Winter

上与天齐——极顶石

Reaching toward the Sky: the Summit Stone

泰山极顶，自有玉皇庙始，便名曰“玉皇顶”。以前是古代祭天的地方。人们认为它与天最近，最容易接近昊天上帝。

“岩岩一片石，上与白云齐。”极顶石，是泰山尊严的象征。它是28亿年前地球的杰作。

极顶石（1956 年）
The Summit Stone (1956)

极顶石（2017 年）
The Summit Stone (2017)

泰山极顶——玉皇顶
The Summit of Mount Tai: the Jade Emperor Peak

The summit of Mount Tai had been named the Jade Emperor Peak since the existence of the Temple of the Jade Emperor, a site where the sacrifice to Heaven was held in ancient times. People used to consider it as closest to Heaven, and the easiest way to get close to the God of the Great Heaven.

"The stone rises so high, reaching toward the sky." As a masterpiece of the earth formed 2.8 billion years ago, the Summit Stone symbolizes the dignity of Mount Tai.

巨石拱北——探海石

Huge Rock Arching Northward: the Craning to the Sea Rock

在岱顶日观峰的东侧，有一腾空而立的巨石，倾斜而出，剑指北方，有“拱北石”之称。又因其毗邻峭壁，翘望东海，又名“探海石”。

There is a huge rock standing upright the east of the SunViewing Peak on top of Mount Tai. The rock is of a shape of sword and tilts northward, so it is named the Arching Northward Rock. It is also called the Craning to the Sea Rock for neighboring a cliff and overlooking the East China Sea.

1988 年，中国人民邮政发行了一套泰山特种邮票。其中的“云海日出”，是以探海石为前景的旭日东升图。

2014 年，第二十二次亚太经合组织（APEC）领导人非正式会议在中国北京举行，中国人民邮政特发行一枚带有探海石的邮票。

In 1988, China Post issued a special set of stamps of Mount Tai, including one “Sea of Clouds and the Sunrise”, which is the scene of sunrise with the foreground of the Craning to the Sea Rock.

On 11 December, 2014, the 22nd APEC Economic Leaders’ Meeting was held in Beijing, China, and China Post issued a special stamp with the design of the Craning to the Sea Rock.

1988 年中国人民邮政发行邮票上的探海石图案
The Design of the Craning to the Sea Rock on the Stamp Issued by China Post in 1988

2014 年中国人民邮政发行邮票上的探海石图案
The Design of the Craning to the Sea Rock on the Stamp Issued by China Post in 2014

雄峙天东
Standing Erect East of Heaven

天堑津渡——仙人桥

A Bridge Crossing Natural Chasm: the Immortal Bridge

仙人桥，几块巨石相叠压，形成拱形桥身，故称“仙人桥”。

悬崖壁立，巨石坠空，人们好奇于它的形成。而在地质学家看来，它是一种风化、崩塌作用下的偶然巧合。

不过，这是一个有着亿万年过程的造化。

“仙人去后渡空留”
“Bridge Was Left after the Departure of the Immortal”

The archy bridge of the Immortal Bridge is formed by several overlying huge rocks.

Its peculiar form that cliff rises steeply and huge rocks hang in the air arise much curiosity. In a geological perspective, it is a kind of coincidence under rock weathering and collapse.

However, that is a natural course going through aeons.

仙人桥
The Immortal Bridge

汉柏连理
The Twinned Han Cypresses

汉柏——昂首天外
One of the Cypresses of Han: "Looking beyond the Horizon"

大汉风骨——汉柏连理

Spirit of the Grand Han: the Twinned Han Cypresses

连理柏，为汉武帝祭祀泰山时所植，距今已有 2100 多年的历史。汉武帝当时在泰山植柏千余株，现在的岱庙尚存“挂印封侯”“赤眉斧痕”“古柏老桧”“昂首天外”等汉柏。

The over 2,100-year-old Twinned Cypresses were planted by Emperor Wu of Han when he came to Mount Tai for offering sacrifices to Heaven and Earth. Emperor Wu planted more than 1,000 cypresses in the area, and today, there are still several preserved in the Dai Temple.

清代乾隆皇帝崇奉泰山，在京都的紫禁城，凭着记忆画出了《汉柏连理图》。

时空跨越，千年唱和。

Emperor Qianlong of Qing worshipped Mount Tai, and he drew the *Scene of Twinned Cypresses of the Han Dynasty* from memory in the Forbidden City.

Acrossing time and space, the response stepped over thousand of years.

古柏老桧
The Old Sabina Chinensis

连理汉柏碑刻拓片
The Inscription Rubbing of the Twinned Han Cypresses

地质奇观——彩石溪

Geological Wonder: the Colorful Rock Stream

彩石溪，位于桃花源溪谷中段，因山溪河床遍布五彩缤纷的岩体而得名。彩色的基岩，形成于25亿至28亿年前。在阳光的照耀下，弯弯曲曲的溪水就像五彩的飘带，斑驳陆离，绚烂多姿。

彩石溪
The Colorful Rock Stream

The Colorful Rock Stream is located in the middle of the Peach Blossom Valley, named for the colorful rocks spreading all over the bed of the stream, which were formed about 2.5 to 2.8 billion years ago. In the sunlight, the winding stream flows just like colorful streamers, shining with variegated brilliance.

彩石溪瀑布
Waterfall over the Stream

溪水春色
Spring Scenery of the Stream

活力彩石溪
The Vibrant Stream

水中精灵——螭霖鱼
Chilin Fish, Little Spirits in the Water

漫步于彩石溪，不同的想象、不同的视觉感受会迎面而来。

Meandering along the stream, you will be greeted with different imaginations and visual enjoyment.

泰山特有物种螭霖鱼，就生长在这彩色的溪水中。神山有神水，神水孕神鱼，为彩石溪增添了一丝灵动。

The Chilin Fish, a species native to Mount Tai, lives in the colorful stream. There is sacred water flowing in the sacred mountain, and sacred fish bred in the sacred water. The fish just adds a streak of ethereality to the water.

人在石上走，画在水下流
People walk on the Rocks, and Pictures Flow under the water

荷叶田田
Thick, Thick Lotus Leaves

醉心
中州單養豪書

奇石之谜——醉心石

Myth of Strange Rock: the "Heart Concentrated" Stele

"醉心"，是17世纪文人的手笔，得悟于其中的人文意象。

在最近的一次同位素测定中，醉心石的年龄被界定在17亿至18亿年左右。

The two characters "Zui Xin" literally meaning "heart concentrated", are the handwriting of a literatus in the 17th century, which was enlightened by the humanistic image therein.

According to the most recent isotope assay, the "heart concentrated" stele is around 1.7 to 1.8 billion years old.

"醉心石"刻石
The "Heart Concentrated" Stele

“小洞天”风韵
Charm of the “Little Fairy Mountain”

即便到了科技发达的今天，人们对这种“桶状构造”地质成因的认识仍然是一知半解。古人在这里题刻“小洞天”，以表达另一种不同一般的神秘。

Even till today when science and techonology are quite advanced, there is only a smattering of knowledge acquired about this kind of "barrel structure". The ancients inscribed "Little Fairy Mountain" here to express another kind of unusual mystery.

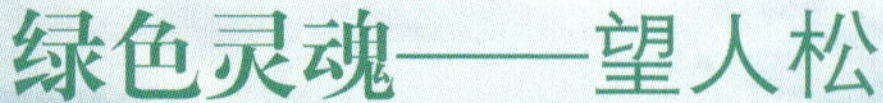

绿色灵魂——望人松

Green Soul: the Guest-Greeting Pine

望人松，位于中天门景区五松亭西侧的山坡上。它树身前探，长枝伸出，如同热情的主人，趋步向前，伸开长臂，迎接泰山的来客。

1987年，望人松被列入世界遗产古树名木保护名录。

The Guest-Greeting Pine is located on the mountain slope west of the Five Pines Pavilion in scenic area of the Midway Gate to Heaven. Its trunk extends forward and its long branches reaches out, just like a gracious host stepping forward with open arms for welcoming visitors to Mount Tai.

In 1987, the Guest-Greeting Pine was listed in the protection list of ancient trees and rare wood species in World Heritage.

探海松
The Exploring the Sea Pine

子母松
The Mother-child Pine

泰山古松，大多集中在山阴的后石坞。姊妹松，并列生长在悬崖上，双株挺秀，相依相偎，婀娜多姿，傲霜斗雪，2005 年版的 5 元人民币上就有她的身影。兄弟松、翔鹤松、探海松……也都生长在这里。

Ancient pines of Mount Tai are mostly in the Behind the Stone Dock. The tall and beautiful Sisters Pines grow side by side on the cliff defying severe cold, and their figures were printed on the 5 yuan bill in the fifth series CNY banknotes issued in 2005. The famous pines such as the Brothers Pines, the Flying Crane Pine, and the Exploring the Sea Pine all grow in this area.

翔鹤松
The Flying Crane Pine

姊妹松
The Sisters Pines

兄弟松
The Brothers Pines

泰山

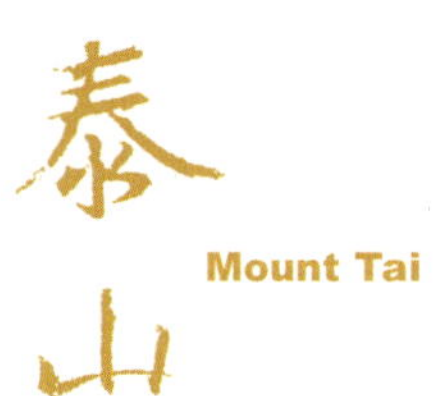

Mount Tai

江山留胜迹

Famous Historical Sites at Mount Tai

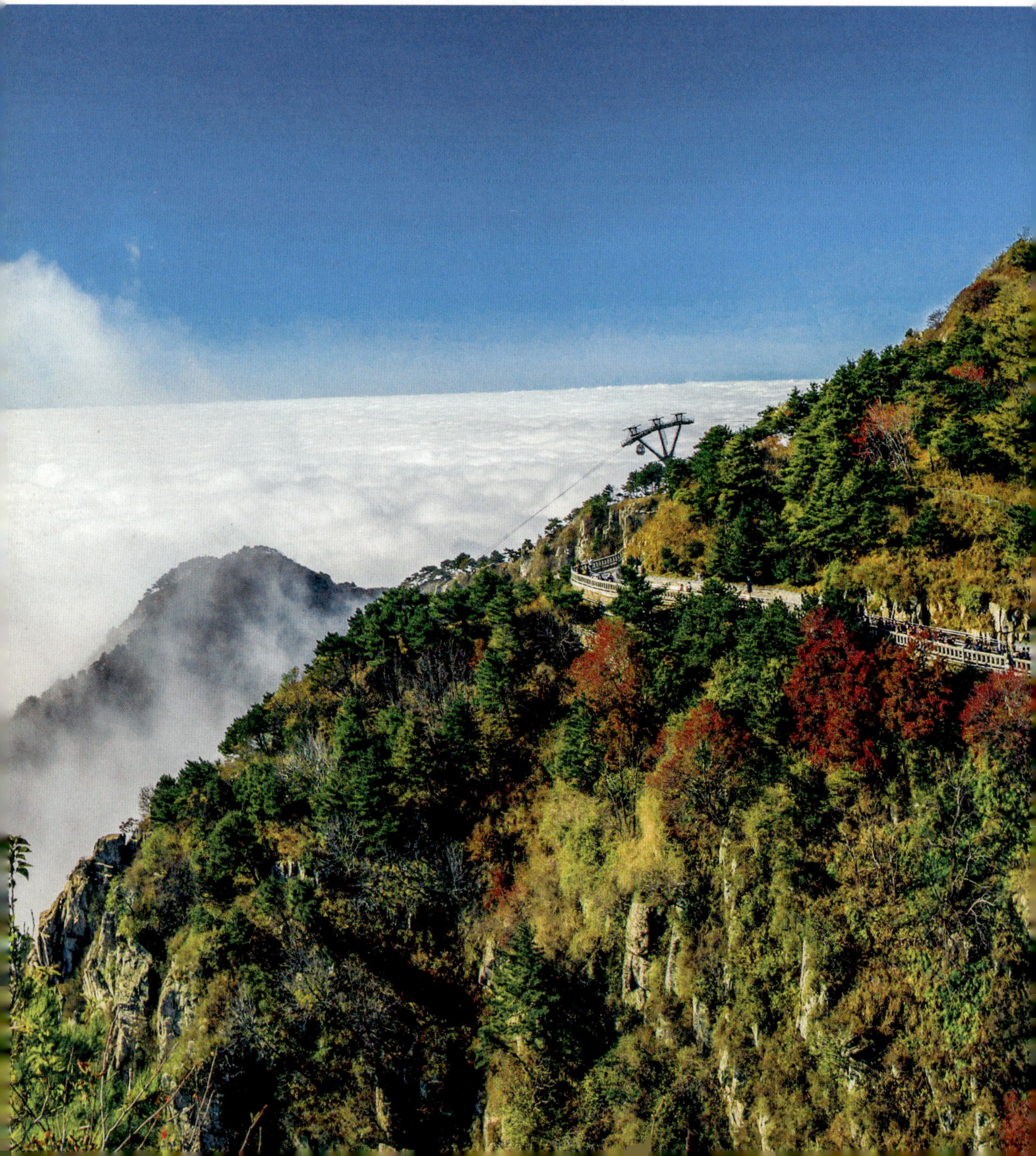

人世变迁，往来古今，后人享受着前人所创造的文化硕果。

As the world changes and time passes, later generations enjoy the cultural fruits created by former generations.

南天门
The South Gate to Heaven

天关之门——南天门

The South Gate of Heaven: Gate of the Pass to Heaven

站在南天门，你会联想到唐代诗人李白“天门一长啸，万里清风来”的诗句，共鸣之情油然而生，只不过当年诗人登临的时候，这扇“门”尚未建置。

一门独启，朝天有路。风范、气势，视觉的、心理的，成功演绎了“登峰造极”的意蕴。

Standing at the South Gate to Heaven, you may think of Li Bai's verses that “A long, long whistle at the Gate to Heaven, Summons refreshing breeze from far, far away”, and a feeling of resonance will arise spontaneously. Only when the poet ascended the mountain, this door had not been built yet.

Opening of the single gate reveals a path to Heaven. The visual and psychological manner successfully interpretes the meaning of “reaching the apex”.

天梯
Ladders to Heaven

南天门近景
Close Shot of the South Gate to Heaven

南天门下十八盘。盘阶结合，道行如梯，是泰山盘道的特色。

There are 18 levels of stairs below the South Gate to Heaven. The path combining with stairs and extending like ladders, are the characteristics of Mount Tai winding path.

中国人民邮政发行邮票中的十八盘
The 18 Levels Stairs on the Stamp Issued by China Post

天门长啸
Long Yell at the Heavenly Gate

天上宫阙——碧霞祠

The Shrine of the Blue Dawn: a Sky Palace

碧霞祠，极顶怀抱，东、西两侧有山峰为屏，南临崖壁，视野开阔。

The Shrine of the Blue Dawn is located at the top of Mount Tai, with the shields of peaks on the east and west sides, and broad vision on the south side as facing the cliff.

坐落于极顶怀中的碧霞祠
The Shrine of the Blue Dawn at the Top of Mount Tai

现悬挂于碧霞祠中的“坤元叶应”“福绥海宇”“赞化东皇”三块大匾，分别由清代的皇帝康熙、雍正、乾隆题写。自明代始，凡泰山朝山进香，必以此庙为先。

朝山进香的香客
Pilgrims Making Pilgrimage to the Shrine

The three horizontal boards hanging in the Shrine of the Blue Dawn, including “Goddess Asisting the Great Deity on Governing the Mountain”, “Blessings Pacifying All the State”, and “Assisting the Transforming and Nourishing Powers of the East Emperor”, are inscribed by Emperor Kangxi, Yongzheng, and Qianlong of the Qing Dynasty respectively. Since the Ming Dynasty, all pilgrims to Mount Tai are bound to worship in the Shrine first.

碧霞祠山门
Gate of the Shrine of the Blue Dawn

碧霞祠“福绥海宇”匾额
The Board “Blessings Pacifying All the State” Inscribed by Emperor Yongzheng of Qing

玉树琼宇
Beautiful Trees and Magnificent Palace